FOR AN ARCHITECTURE OF REALITY

Michael Benedikt

FOR AN ARCHITECTURE OF REALITY

Lumen Books

Lumen Books
446 West 20 Street
New York, NY 10011

© 1987 Lumen, Inc.

Printed in the United States of America
ISBN 0-930829-05-0

Cover: San Miguel de Allende, Mexico
Photograph: Michael Benedikt

Contents

Photographs:

Peter Aron, ESTO: 7 top; Michael Benedikt: 7 bottom, 9, 11 bottom, 15 top and bottom, 35 middle and bottom, 37 top, 39 middle and bottom, 41 top, 43 top, 45 top and bottom, 47 top and bottom, 49 top and middle, 51, 53 top, 55 top, 57 top and bottom, 59 top and bottom, 61 top and bottom, 69; Tom Bernard 55 bottom; Paul Buschong: 43 bottom, 49 bottom, 53 bottom, 67; Paul Caponigro: 11 top, 35 top, 37 bottom; Henri Cartier-Bresson: 39 top, 57 top; Louis Checkman: 13 top; Andrew Duncan 63; John Hejduk: 13 bottom; Pat Lopez: 29 middle; Peter Mauss, ESTO: 27 bottom; Norman McGrath: 17 top and bottom, 29 top; Tim Street Porter: 29 bottom; Cervin Robinson: 17 middle; Stanley Saitowitz: 41 middle and bottom; Robert Schezan: 37 middle; Dudley Witney: 25.

PREFACE

This short book—this extended essay—was written between 1979 and 1984, a period during which historicism and eclecticism, oneiric fictions, nostalgia, irony, and a "scenographic attitude" toward buildings in general spread through architectural education and practice. Over the same period, however, in the visual arts, music, drama, dance, and even literature (where, arguably, post-modernism began), there were signs that the amoral delights of irony, pseudo-history, allusion, pyrotechnic self-reference, and fabulism were wearing thin. In their stead the components of a "New Realism" began to emerge: a taste for veracity and passion, plot and point, texture and straightforwardness, and a renewed respect for realisms of the past.

Today the idea or ideal of "reality" crops up in architecture lecture-circuit presentations with increasing regularity and apparent spontaneity, and it seems that some kind of Realism will eventually come to architecture. If it does not, it will be—I believe—for economic reasons, especially in the United States. "Real buildings" are apt to cost more and/or not look good to a public accustomed to seeing value in the fast construction, ersatz finishes, and "classic" imagery of current high-style architecture. Real buildings are also harder and more costly to design.

I do not claim to propose an eternal philosophy of architecture, just a timely one. I do not claim to suggest how to make buildings beautiful, just more real. I also cannot claim to be a scholar. The ideas in this book are drawn from many sources—from eastern and western religion, from psychology, philosophy, literature, physics, and anthropology, from architecture certainly, from personal experiences, and sources I cannot reliably remember—and I have not been exhaustive in crediting or footnoting the origins of every one. My guides have been the ideas themselves as I understood them and the intuition of what I came to call the "realness" of buildings. If, then, I have unwittingly reiterated some doctrine of the Stoics or misunderstood Heidegger or repeated Kant or not read enough Brentano or Ruskin, I apologize to the scholars. Why? Because I confess to hoping that the directions taken and arguments attempted here might have wider application than to architecture alone.

For their encouragement and criticism over the years, I should like to thank Mauri Tamarin, Roxanne Williamson, Larry Doll, John Pastier, Robert Mugerauer, Horace Newcomb, Suzanne Comer, Nestor Bottino, and Dorothea Scott. The book is dedicated to my late uncle—engineer, inventor, bachelor, and pencil-sketcher extraordinaire—Isaac Solomon, who couldn't stand me doing my homework with the radio on.

Austin, Texas
October 1985

FOR AN ARCHITECTURE OF REALITY

THERE ARE VALUED TIMES in almost everyone's experience when the world is perceived afresh: perhaps after a rain as the sun glistens on the streets and windows catch a departing cloud, or, alone, when one sees again the roundness of an apple. At these times our perceptions are not at all sentimental. They are, rather, matter of fact, neutral and undesiring—yet suffused with an unreasoned joy at the simple correspondence of appearance and reality, at the evident rightness of things as they are. It is as though the sound and feel of a new car door closing with a *kerchunk!* were magnified and extended to dwell in the look, sound, smell, and feel of all things.

The world becomes singularly meaningful, yet without being "symbolical." Objects and colors do not point to other realms, signs say what they have to and fall silent. Conventional associations fall away: a flag against the sky does not conjure a stream of patriotic images—soldiers, funerals, moonwalks—like some TV documentary, but contains in its luminosity and sharp flapping a distilled significance unique to the actual sight and sound of it. We are not conscious ("Ah, this means that . . .") of reference, allusion or instruction. These processes become transparent as their material carriers either disappear, like words, or, like bells and old trees, collapse upon themselves to become crisp and real and, somehow, more the things they are.

Such experiences, such privileged moments, can be profoundly moving; and precisely from such moments, I believe, we build our best and necessary sense of an independent yet meaningful reality. I should like to call them *direct esthetic experiences of the real* and to suggest the following: in our media-saturated times it falls to architecture to have the direct esthetic experience of the real at the center of its concerns.

Compare the following description by Robert Venturi of an award-winning house with a passage from Paul Horgan's novel *Whitewater:*

A Delaware villa, this abundant house . . . [derives] . . . from the 18th century classical barns traditional in Delaware . . . . Taking off from this type, the architects substituted stucco on block for masonry, and flat stylized columns for the chunky Doric order. Above the front pediment, an ornamental screen based on an Austrian Baroque prototype describes the music room behind it while on the other side, a classical lunette screen supported on giant order . . . columns, increases the scale of the house from the valley. The designer's response evokes on a symbolic level the Palladian and Lutyens-like roots of American Country houses. . . . The flat lightweight symbolic ornament eschews pomposity, mixing architectural metaphors and making tongue-in-cheek allusions of great wit.[1]

It's not what they brag about, the lilacs and the green tile dome on the city hall, and the Greek pillars on the bank. No, it's what happens after the sun goes down, and the vapor lights on the tall aluminum poles over the highway come on. Do you think I am raving? . . . You know; the sky is still brilliant, but evening is coming . . . and for the first five minutes or so the vapor lamps have a color . . . and the thing is so magic when it happens it is enough to make you dizzy. Everything on the earth is a sort of gray by then, yes, lilac gray, and there are shadows down the streets, but there, while the sky is changing, those lights are the most beautiful thing in the United States! And you know? It's all an accident! They don't know *how beautiful the light is.[2]*

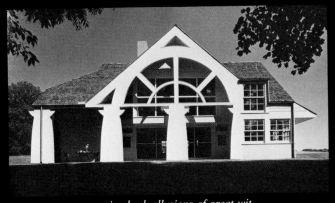

. . . tongue in cheek allusions of great wit.
Flint House, Greenville, Delaware; Venturi, Rauch, and Scott Brown

. . . and there are shadows down the streets . . .
Disch-Falk Field, Austin, Texas

Strategically, Paul Horgan puts into the mouth of an inarticulate teenager words that capture the inarticulable significance of a direct esthetic experience of the real. Here, as in the following excerpt from a poem by Robert Hass, the mundane is blessed:

> *Cat sleeps in the window gleam,*
> *dust motes.*
> *On the oak table*
> *fillets of sole*
> *stewing in the juice of tangerines,*
> *slices of green pepper*
> *on a bone white dish.*[3]

The novel and the poem, though each an act of communication, are windows to a reality empty of the intention to "communicate," a reality neither potential nor ideal, but actual: to a world of things-in-themselves seen clearly. The house as such, on the other hand, seems intended as little more than communication, a knowing and somewhat insolent manipulation of symbols at arm's length to create the "proper" message. If the vapor lights on the aluminum pole are real and have meaning, if the sleeping cat and the white dish are real and have meaning, then they "mean" and are "real" in a quite different way from the way "chunky Doric" or flat and stylized columns "mean" and are "real." How so?

Explicit communications between people aside—such as writing or speech—is the physical world with its beaches and trees, highways and hangars, talking to us? Does something's being meaningful necessarily imply its having something to "say"? Can reality be read like a book or deciphered like a code for its messages? (Which raises the corollary question: if so, from whom are these messages?)

. . . reality empty of the intention to communicate . . .
Room in Woolridge Hall, Austin, Texas

I think not. (At least not literally, in the way, for example, medieval theology after St. Augustine held the world to be God's Book, which the Fall had incapacitated us to read.) It is one thing to recognize that man searches for meaning, but another to say that reality is so obliging as to be, in itself, meaningful. Nor does the earnestness of our search give us license to construct meanings freely. In our time, with more known than ever about the intricate workings of nature and man, is the world still too thin to bear contemplation unfattened by myth or too loose to keep our interest without imposing upon it some easy dramaturgical structure? We seem to fear that unless we keep talking and calling upon the world to talk, we will be overcome by the dread muteness of objects and by the heedlessness of nature, that we might awaken to our "true" condition as "strangers in a strange land."

But, as Ortega y Gasset, Merleau-Ponty, and the existentialists and phenomenologists of this century have pointed out, just being a man or woman and alive is enough to guarantee the world's meaningfulness, and we need not fear. On to any moment of perception—instantly, inevitably and without bidding—the perspective of an entire cultural and biological heritage is brought to bear. Our uprightness is in every tree, rocks divide themselves into the throwable and the not, the future is always ahead. The aluminum poles are cold, the cat warm, the plate clean. Really? Yes. These human facts reverberate with meanings that run deep into our personal yet common histories.

But the objects themselves stand for nothing. Even, or especially, when the world is seen most sensitively, vividly and dispassionately, our humanness is already soaked into it. Just as whipping around to see your back in a mirror is futile, so no objective—that is, non-human—viewpoint, no matter how brief, can be taken with respect to reality. You cannot catch the world unaware and naked of meaning.

. . . just being alive is enough . . .
Blue Ridge Parkway, Virginia

. . . to guaranteee the world's meaningfulness.
Community Hall, Hostyn, Texas

If the search for a vantage point outside the human situation must fail, it represents, nevertheless, a vital and very human desire—even instinct— to know what is really going on apart from our wishes and limitations, to achieve maximum contact with reality-as-is, and to find beauty where it lies. If every thought conjured a reality (a glass of iced tea snaps to hand), the world would rapidly degenerate into a nightmarish Fantasy Island. Here we would meet ourselves over and over again in every face and thing, trapped by our own meager imaginations. In fact, we depend on the world's broad indifference to our designs, its capacity for surprise, and its resistance to our touch for our very sanity. We can find the world inescapably meaningful and real precisely *because* of, and not in spite of, its ''obstinacy''; we must wind our lives around the real and live in its voids and opportunities.

Today, overt and self-conscious fabulation on top of fabulation (in the manner, say, of Italo Calvino or Jorge Luis Borges in literature and, following them, Emilio Ambasz or John Hejduk in architecture), if not confessedly mere beguilement, betrays, I believe, the same impatience with the secrets nature and human nature truly hold from us as that of a boy who, returning from a hunting trip empty-handed, is full of tales built on the tales told by others: of beasts and wizards and knowing trees, of feats and strange inversions. Yes, one can see how vital a role fiction has played in the development of cultures. How could one not? But as John Gardner pointed out,[4] fiction is ultimately to be grounded in our common experience of the world *outside* fiction if, in our cultural life and ultimately our everyday life, we are not to spiral endlessly away from reality.

One quickly sees that allusion, reference, and symbolism in postmodern architecture are comparable to the much-discussed process in postmodern literature, where the blurring of fiction and fact, dazzling effects in the form and surface of the language, take-offs and oblique references to other works and/or the work at hand, manic mythologizing, sly archaism, and, in all, dizzying self-reflection on and in the literary act are typical.

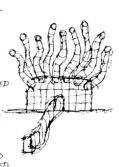

. . . the blurring of fiction and fact . . .

osed fountain for Houston, model, night view with
Emilio Ambasz

24 ARBITRATION HALL

SEE: DEFINITION
FOR THE ARBITRATION OF
DIFFERENCES. THIS HALL
CAN BE CONSIDERED THE
COUNTER-POINT TO THE
MASQUE, ONE INVOLVED
WITH THE JUDICIAL THE
OTHER WITH A SILENT
RITUAL.
THE STRUCTURE IS CONSTRUCTED
OF REINFORCED CONCRETE
(FLOOR SLAB) AND STEEL,
METAL CLAD. THE MEDUSA
LIKE LIGHT-WELLS (OPEN TO
THE WEATHER) LET IN LIGHT
AND ACT AS A VENTING
A SPECIFIC SET OF
INTERIOR ELEMENTS ARE
CONSTRUCTED OF HARD WOODS
AND ARE CAREFULLY FINISHED
IN BEES WAX

LOCATION: NEAR CROSS OVER-BRIDGE

fors. Buildings are what one might call primar
permanent and largely impassive. We should n
the "communicators"—the directors and actor
cians, columnists, photographers, anchor-men a
matter—to the producers, broadcasters and pub
d paper and cable companies enough, and to who
rest in telling us what we want to hear, showing
, and in keeping us tuned in to the collective
cal and mental landscape has become as canvas

for a meaningful architecture, historicist
-classicist postmodern architects inevitably find
ve from any authentic reality and set on a theore
abandoning an architecture that belongs to t
h words, signs, and symbols refer to, for an arc
nselves. Architecture becomes just one more m
ell-intentioned communicators if not just entert
n "information age" it is too easy to lose sight
omething is, is distinct from what it communica
e suppression of the perception of reality in

. . . we count on our buildings to form . . .
Housing, Soweto, South Africa

his lies the fact that buildings designed on the
is a medium of communication cannot hope to
y, direct esthetic experiences of their own realit
ry nature of the direct esthetic experience is suc
lusion and symbolism to what is actually there.

often not a reality with integrity of its own, bu
he reality-of-referents the architect would have

postmodernism had little to do with its proclai
creation of a richer, more complex, more sy
ore humane architecture than was possible on th
n Movement. When architects create plywo
nic columns, or concrete garlands, the arch is no
nor the column a real column, the garland a gar
mply appreciated for the novel things they are. I
Postmodernism's frequent sparkle and sudden
cizing and dandy seriousness do often give rise t
But, as Susan Sontag wrote in *Against Interpr*
. . . as distinct from style, reflects an ambival
icted by contempt, obsession contradicted by iro
natter''[6] that ultimately undermines its own end
er the rush of refreshed vision, and the polemic
find space for the ironic posture that supports
on makes itself felt. One is far from home. One

. . . nor the column a real column
Piazza d'Italia, New Orleans; Charles Moore

. . . or the garland a garland
Public Service Building, Portland, Oregon; Michael Graves

...OR OF MY COMMENTARY thus far may not see
I am thinking not only of recent writings by, say,
rg-Schulz, Christopher Alexander, Aldo van Eyck
, and some others but also of the critical reaction to ne
stmodern work found in the editorial, letters, and co
is of such popular professional journals as *Progressive*
rchitectural Record, and *Architectural Review.* (See A
hope we can now see that "fake," "cute," "ac
ived"—these frequently-used terms of derogation in cr
odernism—and "existential," "place," "authentic
of appeal—all point to something, something missi
gs: a sense of *reality.*

Today, when it is almost universally agreed that what you see is not what you get, it seems rather naive to speak of "one reality" or intuitions thereof. The "world," most sophisticated people believe, is an ever evolving, socially constructed, personally projected solution to (what can one say?) the problems of existence. It is therefore fundamentally "relative." And only by maintaining this Idealist doctrine, we believe, are we able to fully exercise our "human potential": life, *your* life, and with it reality, "your reality," is what you make of it. And so, unceasingly distracted by data, media events, opinions, advertisements, and entertainments all conspiring to interchangeability, able to appeal to recent scientific thinking which, from physics to sociology, champions neutrality with regard to frames of reference and even the a priori "unknowability" of reality,[7] persuaded deeply of the psychological worldview, and, furthermore, righteous about the humanism of it all . . . it is small wonder that one can hardly write the word "reality" without quotation marks any more (or say it without them either).

Even pragmatist William James, the only psychologist I know of who addressed our sense of reality as such (did he know it would come under threat?), advanced the "many worlds" argument,[8] that is, the idea that there is not one world but many, right here: the world of physical things, the world of scientific concepts, the world of myths, the world of chess . . . and so on, each with its own "style of existence" and each of which, he argued, was as real as the strength of our *belief* in it. The strength of this belief in turn is based upon (*a*) what good it does us to believe it, (*b*) its internal logical consistency, and (*c*) its not conflicting with external "facts," *i.e.* other beliefs and worlds.

This view strikes us as contemporary. We think of ourselves in various roles in various worlds as a matter of course now: there is the world of work, the world of home and family, of sport, of religious observance, the world of your choice within the world of television, and so on. And if amongst these worlds, these roles, these selves, we search vainly for the "real us," it is not because there is no real us but because we have come to believe more deeply that all-the-world's-being-a-stage precludes the very possibility.

And yet, and yet. While professing "many-worldism" and changing our clothes, while nodding at how mercurial are the truths of science (and therefore everything else), we are actually one-worldists to a man when it comes to a good cup of coffee.

A touch on our shoulder: we are here. So familiar is the ring of truth, the tenor of reality, the "bite and sweet gravity" (Sontag) of things real and beautiful that if we are, most of us, as I surmise, fairly expert at discerning what is really real from what is not, then there lies here a tragedy of some proportion: we will not claim the expertise for fear of appearing unworldly.

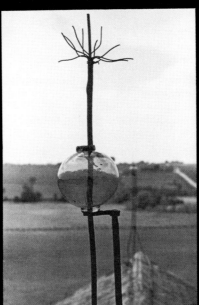

Lightning rod on a barn in Ontario. The farmer knows his barn was struck. Tendrils gathered, a new purple glass ball is slipped on and—without deliberation—the wires spread, to wait again.

Barn, Moltke, Ontario

SO WHAT TO DO? I have spoken of the direct esthetic experience of the real. Can one analyze this experience? Can one analyze what makes up our sense of the real? Can so all-encompassing and portentous a word as "reality" be found to apply to architecture in anything but a trivial way? I think so; and I believe there are directions for the future to be found in continuing our exploration.

One can begin by noting that certain parts of reality and certain times in the ongoing stream of events are commonly considered less than, or other than, "really real." Dreams, for example. Dreams are real, of course, but we deal with them in ways that show that we understand their rather special status and relationship to everyday reality. There are other, more interesting cases: games, illusions, jokes, rehearsals, re-enactments, magic, deceptions . . . , each set aside or bracketed from "reality-proper" differently and for different reasons. One turns to Erving Goffman for the analysis these cases deserve, especially in his book *Frame Analysis.*[9]

And then there is art. Art's relationship to reality is surely the most difficult one about which to theorize conclusively. The very problem is an eternal subject for art, and the rewards for progress while eluding capture by theory are high.

Early chapters of Arthur Danto's recent book *The Transfiguration of the Commonplace*[10] examine the ways in which art is not real, and conclude that the relationship between art and reality is one of "aboutness." How does one part of reality, art, come to be regarded as being characteristically about the rest? By the way artworks are "framed," that is, by the avowed intentions and behavior of the artist, the gallery or stage in which they are placed (or the deliberate non-placement of the work in a gallery or on stage), by the critical exegesis of historians, critics, dealers, peers . . . in short, by the way works are taken by virtue of being in the "artworld."

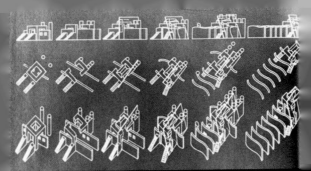

an Architecture of Games
from "The Manhattan Transcripts"; Bernard Tschumi

an Architecture of Dreams
"Emilio's Folly: Man Is an Island"; Emilio Ambasz

an Architecture of Illusions
Mural, Kroger Building, Cincinnati; Richard Haas

In such a view, a piece of architecture, to be art, must enter the artworld and fulfill its responsibilities there. It must be envisaged, be presented, be posed—framed—as art is, and be *about* something. Again, the psychic and professional rewards are high, and success is rare: the process is one of utmost seriousness and demanding of extraordinary skill. Given, then, a "thrust toward art" by architects, that is, a striving toward achieving the particular and difficult "unreality" of art, and given the likelihood of missing the mark in the attempt, are we not likely to find all the "un-realities" represented in the recent history of architecture? We should be able to discern: an Architecture of Dreams, an Architecture of Games, an Architecture of Illusions, an Architecture of Enactments (pre- and re-), an Architecture of Jokes, and so on.

This still leaves the desideratum of architecture-as-art. From our perspective, however, even architecture-as-art and art-as-aboutness seem to be ideas that together lead away from reality and an "Architecture of Reality"—or *real architecture*—too. We must either drop "art" and assign to real architecture a special aboutness of its own, or we must drop the requirement of aboutness entirely, and have architecture simply "be itself" without being about anything. In the latter case, we might wish to retain the idea of architecture-as-art and claim that, Danto to the contrary, art too, can just "be." On reflection though, one despairs of the possibility of an art or an architecture that can just "be" without being about "just being." And perhaps, framing creatures that we are, that is the best we can hope for.

an Architecture of Jokes
Commercial Building, Austin, Texas; Arquitectonica

an Architecture of Re-enactment
Jniversity of Houston School of Architecture Building, Houston, Texa
Philip Johnson

an Architecture of Pre-enactment
Centre Pompidou, Paris, France; Piano and Rogers

Which brings us back to the possibility of an architecture with a special aboutness of its own. We find ourselves close to being able to answer the question: what then is "real architecture"? and its corollary (if one is unwilling to give up architecture-as-art), how can architecture be art and reality simultaneously?

At this point it seems safe to say that, first, real architecture is architecture especially ready—so to speak—for its direct esthetic experience, an architecture that does not disappoint us by turning out in the light of that experience to be little more that a vehicle contrived to bear meanings; and, second, real architecture, if it must inevitably be an architecture about something (at least from the perspective of a designer or critic) is about being (very) real. This, if you will, is its "special aboutness."

Real architecture is, then, architecture in which the quality of *realness* is paramount. And here, with realness, is how the idea of reality can best enter the realm of architectural discourse. Like "proportion" or "scale," like any number of qualities ascribable to architecture good and bad, "realness" becomes an attribute of buildings that can be pointed out and discussed, can be found lacking here, present in greater degree there . . . and so on: in short, realness becomes an observable quality amenable to some level of conceptual formulation.

What remains to be done in this essay is to explore, necessarily in outline, the components of realness; the whole enterprise to be carried out in the light and memory of direct esthetic experiences of the real, which are fundamental and which form the guiding intuition.

REALNESS, I THINK, CAN BE divided into four components, the last one of which has two aspects:

presence,

significance,

materiality, and

emptiness (emptiness$_1$, emptiness$_2$).

Each contributes to realness more or less independently: a lack of one (say, materiality) does not imply a lack of another (say, significance). Rather, weakness or absence of one component leads to diminution of the summative effect that is realness. By the same token, the powerful presence of one component might compensate—if you will—for the weakness of another.

Presence may be understood in the trivial sense. After all, if you can see it and touch it, it has presence in as much as it exists to the senses. But here presence means something more than merely being perceptible; something, rather, analogous to the "presence" attributed to certain people—stage presence in an actor, for instance—or to "presence of mind." Implied is a certain tautness, attentiveness, assertiveness.

A building with presence, for example, is not apologetic, but asserts itself as architecture, having a right to be here, to bump off a few trees (and defer to others), to take up its position as a new entity in the physical world. A building with presence is not one that would wish to disappear (as do underground, camouflage/contextual, and some mirror-glass buildings); nor is it coy, silly, garbled, embarrassed, referential, nervous, joking, or illusory—all attempts at getting away from being here now.

Staircase, San Francisco

Street signs, Fort Sumner, New Mexico

The
OLD BORUNDA
CAFE

r building (or person) with presence has a shine,
metry to it. Well-constructed, though perhaps a
ean, though its paint may be peeling, its presence
nly visually, but also by coherent appeal to othe
ement, sound, smell. Edges are distinct just as o
Articulated parts are not so much adjacent or lin
d, just as the whole does not shamble, fill, a
sely where it needs to be and ends there. Every n
ully itself and revealed. From the flare on the
ple to the chain that drips pearls of rain, from
e Parthenon to its subtly curved steps in the su
very kind have been devised to "bring out" a
ts harmonics. All in the service of presence.

with presence, with a kind of mute awareness
d windows open, finally seems attentive to *ou*
patient, surrounding us with a benign otherness
Heidegger put it. Dimensioned and hinged just so
waits for our return.

. . . edges are distinct . . .
Market Hall, Plum, Texas

. . . stands precisely where it needs to be . . .
Building One, Buenos Aires, Argentina; Agrest and Gandelsonas

. . . enhancements of every kind . . .
Roof, Hiei-San, Japan

If presence is largely a perceptual matter, *significance* is a cognitive one. (I intend the term in its least technical sense, closer to "important" as in "Jack was a significant person in my life" or as in "significant event," than to the semiotic process of signifying itself, as in "the significance of the thumbs-down gesture survives to this day.") Significance is not achieved by the display of icons, signs and symbols—no matter how "appropriate"—but by how buildings actually come to be and how they continue to be part of the lives of the people who dream them, draw them, build them, own them, and use them.

Buildings with significance are significant *to someone,* rather than, or in addition to, being symbolic *of something.* Symbols and icons function in the context of *ritual*; significant objects and places need not be so framed. (It follows that designers and theorists interested in architectural symbolism would find themselves drawn to ritual building-types, such as crematoria or libraries, and/or bound to treat ritualistically and with unwarranted piety the most everyday routines and environments. Pyramids over everything perform offhand consecrations, every east window creates an Axis or Rebirth rather than a place to sprout beans, and every stair is an Ascent to Heaven rather than to upstairs.) Symbols can be non-significant, things can be significant and not be symbolic; between symbolism and significance, significance has the existential import and is the larger category.

. . . and how they continue . . .
"Last Days of the Kuomintang," Beijing

. . . to be part of . . .
Elementary School, San Miguel de Allende, Mexico

. . . the lives of people.
Church, Playa del Carmen, Mexico

For example, while no one would contest that a medieval bell tower was a fine and meaningful architectural element, "putting one in," say, a shopping center inevitably subverts its symbolic power. If the bell tower arrived by flatbed and crane, then, for all the useful things that it does (bong on the hour, orient shoppers), its significance will always include the lack of correspondence between its true history and its "historicity," a lack that nags at and hollows the swell of nostalgia it begins. Iconic scenography as a mode of architectural design rests on cynicism about the very possibility of authenticity. When inauthenticity is seen as harmless and/or as the inevitable outcome of applying creative energy to a design problem, then cynicism becomes a necessary professional posture never quite cloaked by any amount of wit and winsomeness.

No, a new building is given historical significance over and above its formal timeliness only if it brings to light the genuine history—human or natural—of its site and the circumstances of its construction. Significant buildings, real buildings, are achieved rather than provided. They are built over time by someone rather than arriving all but ready-made by strangers. Thus we should not be surprised at how often anonymous buildings, *provided* by government or "housing authority," or *provided* by corporations, are neglected, vandalized, or just suffered and ignored.

Buildings with significance show a fundamental seriousness—even when they are "follies"—and a sense of magnitude independent of their actual size. Their good workmanship forms a bond, in the manner of a gift, between the designer/owner/builder and the user, no matter how modest the scale and materials. Effort, care, ingenuity (rather than cleverness), knowledge, ambition—these traits of its creators "come through" in a building and tell us how it is to be taken.

. . . the history of its site
"Co-op," near San Angelo, Texas

. . . achieved rather than provided.
Roof, Brebnor House, Transvaal, South Africa; Stanley Saitowitz

. . . a sense of magnitude . . .
Catherine House, Transvaal, South Africa; Stanley Saitowitz

Certain buildings gather to themselves a credibility by the above factors alone. Impervious and silent—as clouds pass over, days of rain and hail, as generations are born and die—St. Peter's Basilica, for example, exists now as an almost incomprehensibly massive investment of human effort, material resources, and time, one that transcends any judgment about its beauty or worth. Such monumental buildings quite literally define what *is*. But to some extent all buildings share in their power simply for being architecture. One can see how buildings constructed rapidly by indifferent men with indifferent plans, using remotely made and general parts, are bound to create indifference—at best—in the population at large, let alone in those actually involved. These buildings lack significance to anyone, and are the less real for it.

. . . a bond, in the manner of a gift . . .
House under construction, Austin, Texas; Michael Benedikt

. . . indifferent men with indifferent plans . . .
Condominiums under construction, Austin, Texas

Materiality is probably the least problematic of the four components. It reflects our intuition that for something to be real it ought to be (made of) "stuff," material having a paplability, a temperature, a weight and inertia, an inherent strength. (Hence our native skepticism of the "reality" of radio waves, quarks, dreams, and space.) The appeal for materiality, however, is not an appeal for heaviness of materials. The dark and corded tents of the Beduoin are no less material than the stone vaults of a 14th-century French monastery.

Part of our appreciating the materiality of an object has to do with our appreciation of the natural origin of its substance and the manufacturing or forming processes that the latter has evidently undergone. New and very synthetic materials are confusing in this way: neither their origin nor their forming is readily perceivable. This makes materiality the component of realness most often implicated when something is judged to be "fake," though the term applies also, in more difficult-to-discuss ways, to the other components. Veneers are fake if and when they suggest solidity and consistency of material throughout the piece. (When they do not, they may function, and be seen to function, as casings, crusts, or skins.) Most plastic veneers are doubly fake: they disguise not only the lack of correspondence between surface and interior, but also the nature of the material in the first place, like a decoy. The ubiquity of gypsum wallboard ("drywall") construction derives, of course, from the speed, economy, and formal freedom with which walls and ceilings of eye-fooling substantiality can be made. Essential to its success, however, is drywall's visual similarity to plastered masonry (still, somehow, the "real thing" even after all these years) and the fact that we cannot tirelessly remain aware of the difference.

. . . a palpability, a temperature . . .
Carpenter's Hall, Philadelphia, Pennsylvania; Robert Smith

. . . casings, crusts, or skins . . .
"Petal House," Santa Monica, California; Eric Owen Moss

Technically speaking, a material is fake when it displays some but not all of the qualities of the material we take it to be. And it is the selecting of qualities that "will do" from the complex of qualities properly belonging to the real stuff that, together with the dissemblance, indicates what Sartre would have called "bad faith" on the part of the designer/provider toward the user/appreciator . . . unless, that is, the deception is *framed* as such. For example, almost all the architecture of fantasy depends on a deceptive materiality. This can be made acceptable and enjoyable, though only to the extent that the suspension of disbelief is willing. Disneyland has gates, movie palaces have doors, and if, within, they are not entirely believable, they are at least leave-able.

For all this, one cannot realistically suggest that buildings be of "all natural" material, the way Frank Lloyd Wright or the architects of the Arts and Crafts Movement might have wished. The forces of economics, the age-old desire of clients to have more precious materials and effects than they can afford (together with the ambitions of architects along these same lines), the existence of an enormous body of precedents that includes some of our most revered examples of fine architecture (Palladio's stucco/stone, for example)—all these make an insistence on authenticity in materials somewhat quixotic. There are three ways "out."

The first is to follow the 1915 advice of Geoffrey Scott, who seemed to recognize the impending renewal of the problem's importance. He simply advised moderation and common sense, and would have been pleased with, say, Grand Central Terminal in New York.[11] Like the majority of large Beaux Arts buildings, this framework of iron and steel was seamlessly clad in a stone veneer. Of considerable mass in itself however (unlike the three-quarter-inch thick granite facings we bolt from behind onto our office towers), the stone retains most of the structural and material exigencies that characterize solid masonry construction. Although the massiveness and materiality suggested by the classical form of the building as a whole is orders of magnitude greater than its actual mass, he would have found the building, as we surely do, "material enough," in spite of the deception.

. . . suspension of disbelief . . .
Getty Museum, Santa Monica, California

. . . material enough.
State Legislative Buildings, Olympia, Washington; Wilder and White

The other two "ways out" are or were essentially modernist strategies, finding early expression at the turn of the century primarily in the work and essays of Adolf Loos.[12] The first is to use materials, no matter how allusive, *as* allusive, and to seize upon the genuinely unique properties of the material: to show the thickness of veneer, the hollowness of gypsum-board walls, the marvel of formica marble, the freedom and power of paint. This addresses the issue of authenticity by framing, by making fakery honest, as it were. (One must be wary, however, of covertly believing the lie while overtly admitting deceit.)

The second strategy consists in *(a)* eschewing materials that do not look or behave like what they are, *(b)* using materials that have keen tactile, visual, and kinesthetic qualities—shiny or veined or sawn, *(c)* structurally stressing materials so that, in feeling "their pain," we are drawn to consider their substance, and *(d)* not using materials that look or feel like nothing in particular (whose material is immaterial, as it were). The last point is important. For indeterminacy of material detracts from realness as much as fakery. The term "ticky-tacky" expresses well not only our disdain for the (supposed) cheapness of a material, but our defeat at identifying it.

Clarity in what a building is made of, how it is made on that account, and how the way it looks reflects both, are all essential, then, to a building whose realness is to derive in full measure from materiality. The case of ruins and very old buildings is illustrative. Here, wear and signs of maintenance, cracks and collapses, reveal all; and when this clarity of *materiality* is joined by *presence* and *significance,* the *realness* of these structures becomes indelible.[13] But there is one more component to realness that explains the power of ruins and of the many fine vernacular buildings (and those rare designed ones) that stand so unblinkingly and enigmatically in the light of our ratiocinations about them: *emptiness.*

. . . tactile, visual, and kinesthetic . . .
"Farmer's Lumber Co.," La Grange, Texas

. . . our defeat at identifying it.
Library at San Juan Capistrano, California; Michael Grav

. . . cracks and collapses reveal all.
Water-wheel ruin, New Braunfels, Texas

The word "emptiness" has a set of connotations not intended here—that sick and hollow feeling of loss or loneliness, the pain of hunger, and so forth. What is meant by emptiness here is rather more like . . . silence, clarity, and transparency. Emptiness may resound without sound, may be filled by its potential to be filled, and make open what is complete. . . . Yes, emptiness is surely the most difficult component of realness with which to deal verbally, yet perhaps the most important one. Very much an intuition, it can be analyzed only up to a point, and suggestiveness in the language is more necessary than ever.

. . . may resound without sound . . .
Pike Place Market, Seattle, Washington; G. R. Bartholick

I think that two distinct types or aspects of emptiness are discernible, related to each other, I can only say, somehow. *Emptiness*₁ is approximated by words such as "artlessness," "innocence," "suchness," "quiddity," "inevitability," "unworldliness," "purposelessness"— all terms indicating the "emptiness of intention" we attribute to nature. The appeal to nature as a model in architectural theory is fundamentally the search for *realness* through emptiness or through emulating God's work, both of which share the property of being beside or beyond human wilfulness and intelligence, and thus definitive of an independent, base reality upon which and within which life is managed. Nature is patient, ever-productive, and disinterested in the results the way no man or woman can be. This lends to natural objects the paradoxical qualities of both arbitrariness and inevitability. Teleological/functional explanations of, say, the patterns on butterfly wings are childish: the flower does not bloom so that we can enjoy its fragrance, nor does it rain in order to slake the thirst of animals. As the Zen haiku has it:

> *departing geese do*
> *not intend their reflection*
> *in the lake below.*[14]

For architecture, emptiness₁ implies that a building should not be slave to its program, twisting and turning to accommodate our every movement and wish—squirming to please, as it were—but rather should be formed according to innate principles of order, structure, shelter, the evolution of architecture itself—and accident. It should be *found* useful and beautiful, like a tree. The dumb and inexplicable features of old and/or vernacular buildings, otherwise so straightforwardly organized, are often precisely those that attract us to inhabit them. Offering opportunity rather than giving direction, they are indifferent to our designs on them. They were there before us, they are "wrong" in a way that challenges us to possess them creatively: they seem realer if not "better" than anything we could design from scratch, and that is why, increasingly, we like them.

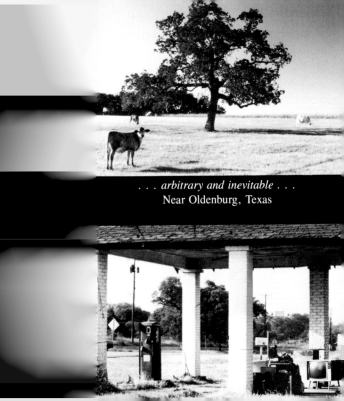

. . . *arbitrary and inevitable* . . .
Near Oldenburg, Texas

How hard it is to design egolessly; form without rhetoric, without artifice, pretension, or dragging surplus. Few architects have succeeded, and then only in maturity. Louis Kahn was one who strove publicly to do so and succeeded at the Kimbell Art Museum in Fort Worth and the Salk Institute at La Jolla. Kahn's word for emptiness was "Silence," and indeed, to experience the open, cycloid vaults that enfront the Kimbell is to hear Silence. ("You know what is so wonderful about those porches?" he said of them, "They're so unnecessary.") Mies van der Rohe's search for anonymity and stylelessness was prompted by the same insight but crippled by adherence to the ideal of rationality and a certain megalomania, while Adolf Loos had arrived at "silence" long before: the meaning and "language" of architecture, he asserted, was to be nothing other than building itself—the materials and techniques of construction, sensuous and unadorned, brought to limpid perfection.[15]

Two strains are to be found in the work of Robert Venturi: on the one hand a willful, almost perverse delight in tackiness and proletarian taste-excesses, on the other a striving for the dumbness, happy wrongness, "just-so-ness"—realness—of vernacular architecture. Now, the former may indeed be like the popular architecture of the strip and suburb and in this sense "realistic," but this architecture is itself unreal in the sense I have been discussing it, and *referring* to it merely adds another layer of unrealness. From this corpus of Venturi's work, from certain passages in *Complexity and Contradiction in Architecture* and then *Learning from Las Vegas,* comes the license we see in postmodernism to which I, and Venturi himself, have objected. But the second strain of work—bricky, slightly odd, direct yet somehow confounding, a line of work culminating in his excellent Gordon Wu Hall at Princeton University—comes closer to having emptiness, and, I believe, comes closer to exemplifying what Venturi had in mind in *Complexity and Contradiction.*

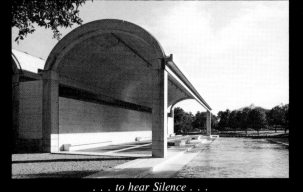

. . . to hear Silence . . .

Kimbell Art Museum, Fort Worth, Texas; Louis Kahn

. . . direct yet somehow confounding . . .

Gordon Wu Hall, Princeton, New Jersey; Venturi, Rauch, and Scott Brown

Emptiness₂ is more akin to the idea of space, or interval. The Japanese have the word *ma* which comes close to the meaning of *emptiness* intended here. *Ma!* Ma is in the gaps between stepping stones, in the silence between the notes in music, in what is made when a door slides open. When a child's swing reaches the point of neither rising nor falling and is momentarily weightless . . . there is ma. Yet emptiness₂ is ma and something else. When we speak of the "draw" of a good fireplace, when we feel the pull of an empty room for us to enter and dwell there, when we see in something incomplete the chance for continuation or find in things closed a gate . . . there is *emptiness₂*.

Kahn again provides an example. Beneath the Kimbell's porch vaults we are drawn up—inhaling, sailing—with them. And in the rhythm of the other vaults—identical sisters but closed—these open ones beg the air for yet more. At the Salk, the pearlescent plaza with its central water course and radical tensile openness draws together the sea just beyond the hills and the sky overhead. We lift up our eyes, and our spirit is made to lie down. . . . How different is this emptiness, this silence, from the silence that pervades so much of the work of the Neo-Rationalists. Theirs is the silence of a graveyard, the surreal airlessness of a de Chirico painting, where architectural forms—closed, mute and banal—have us believe not that they are pregnant with ineffable significance, but that we are suddenly deaf.

. . . in the space between . . .
"Behind the Gare Saint-Lazare," Paris

. . . to pull to enter . . .
Pike Place Market, Seattle, Washington; G. R. Bartholick

. . . the sea just beyond . . .
Salk Institute, La Jolla, California; Louis Kahn

John Dewey[16] had explained esthetic feeling as the satisfaction derived from the neat opening and closing of an experience framed and orchestrated by an artist. Rare in everyday life (which is perpetually unresolved) esthetic experiences are especially valued, all the more for supporting as they do belief in the possibility of symmetry and justice in the design of the world as a whole. It is not inaccurate, I think, to say that Dewey's ideas are widely held to explain adequately what is nice about Art and why we ought to have it. Emptiness$_2$ calls for something different. Emptiness$_2$, component of realness that it is, is more like life as we find it, and points us towards the beauty in life's openness and beckoning: in window gleam, in dust motes on an oak table. Architecture with emptiness$_2$ is thus always unfinished: if not literally, then by the space it makes and the potential it shows. We become engaged with the intervals and open ends.

. . . the space it makes . . .
 mentary school, San Miguel de Allende, M

The urge is strong to make a building complete in itself and finished, a totally encompassing, dazzling, climate-controlled and conditioned experience. But totality and completeness are too often achieved at the expense of realness. For all their presence and materiality, the four-square composure of a Palladian villa or surburban house by Mario Botta can seem smug and contrived: the buildings not themselves but portraits of themselves—impervious, imperious, and ideal. And at the other end of the design spectrum, achieving another sort of self-sufficiency, shopping malls and ''Portmanesque'' hotels with their tubbed ficus trees under air-conditioned daylight, their tireless escalators, water-works, and constant, faintly reverberating clamor, are little short of pre-enactments of life aboard a space colony.

Not unlike the malls, much contemporary high-style architecture lacks emptiness$_2$ by being quite literally full. Full, if not of people and goods and pushy displays, then of Design. Ramps and catwalks, columns and rails, steps and grids and stepped grids, skylit crevasses, small things too big, big things too small, nineteen colors, composed furniture, art and more art, rotunda, little pyramids, pediment pieces, Arcadian tableaux, spaces within spaces within spaces overlaid and layered four deep with thin walls and theories, architectural origami . . . no room is left for us to enter. Here, in fact, both emptiness$_1$ and emptiness$_2$ come together in their lack. For these buildings are not only full of things coming and going, they are full of themselves and their cleverness.

. . . imperious, impervious, and ideal . . .
Villa Foscari, Malcontenta, Italy; Andrea Palladio

Kite on the beach, Venice, California

HERE, THEN, ARE THE COMPONENTS of realness: *presence, significance, materiality,* and *emptiness.* Certainly these, or something very close to them, are the "true" constituents of our intuition of realness or, conversely, the attributes of things physical and real to us.

Over and above the merits of this particular analysis, however, I am convinced that the type of phenomenological enquiry attempted here is essential for architectural theory. For in recent years, architectural theory as an enterprise has become almost entirely historiographical in its outlook and methods. Having strayed from a long and venerable course, the efforts of the Moderns to be of or ahead of their time—to re-think architecture, its ends and means—have come to be seen as the very cause of their demise, and it is small wonder that eclecticism and historicism and "mythicism" now tempt us.

For all its failings, however, the Modern Movement represented a profound ideological, technological and economic shift in the way buildings were, and are, regarded and built—one that cannot be wished away, "historicized," or dealt with regretfully. While it may be argued that ironic poses and movie-set history, allegories and recondite allusions, reflect most accurately and properly our information- and entertainment-oriented culture, they can also be seen as a defeat: a sliding of architecture into the world of television. For it can be argued equally well that an architecture that stands against, or in contrast to, the culture-wide trend to ephemeralization and relativism—as a kind of last bastion of dumb reality and foil to it all—constitutes the more appropriate, timely, and potentially more esthetic response. This, of course, is my position, and my plea.

Czeslaw Milosz arrived in Paris one summer morning in 1931. In his autobiography he describes it thus:

Four or five o'clock. Grey-pink irridescent air like the enamel inside a shell. We inhaled Paris with open nostrils, cutting across it on foot, diagonally from the north towards the Seine. The moist flowers, the vegetables, the coffee, the damp pavement, the mingling odors of night and day. . . . We lost count of the streets, we forgot about our own existence . . . the promise was infinite, it was the promise of life.[17]

If I needed an "-ism" for the architecture I have variously called "real architecture" and "the architecture of reality," and if New Modernism were not enough, then, with Milosz and Horgan's teenager, Philipson Durham,[18] stoned on realness, I would call it "High Realism." This would describe not only architecture designed now to have the special quality of realness, but also countless buildings, mostly anonymous, which, like those painted by Richard Estes, capture us by their presence, significance, materiality and emptiness.[19]

Shed near Marble Falls, Texas

High Realism: undoubtedly an architecture easier to call for than to master, easier to find than to produce. Its inspiration lies in an elusive esthetic experience as precious as it is rare in our media-soaked age: the direct esthetic experience of the real.

If we cannot grasp reality as a whole or even be sure that we have in part, we seem nonetheless to be allowed glimpses. We know it to be "at hand." And the quality of realness that certain objects, people and places have more than others leads us on, like a scent, a promise, evidence.

San Miguel de Allende, Mexico

APPENDIX

Words in boldface are from *Roget's Thesaurus'* listing for "unreal." All non-boldface words are quoted from letters-to-the-editor critical of post-modernism in the following Journals, from 1975-1985: *AIA Journal* (now *Architecture*), *Progressive Architecture, Crit,* and *Architectural Record.* Also included are quotations from the annual state-of-architecture review essays from the *AIA Journal.*

Terms and phrases in quotation marks were either non-grammatical or quotable, if awkward, inventions by the authors. Words in parentheses are my own or the authors, and help to indicate the context of the term or the sense in which it was used. Most terms were found more than once (especially counting grammatical variations): "fad," "fake," symbolic," "kitsch," "stageset," and "allusion" leading with more than 10 mentions each. No attempt was made to put all terms into adjectival form. They are as found.

The pejorative terms listed below account for the vast majority of critical epithets and phrases found, omitting only *(a)* judgments of untimeliness and non-progressiveness, and *(b)* terms of general disapproval and distaste ("ugly," "bad", "awful," and so on), neither of which has to do with reality/unreality as such. I do not claim that a list as long as this and having, perhaps, some unifying sense of its own (probably based on the notions of "sterility" and "scale") could not be compiled from critiques of Modernism. I claim only to show here an almost complete correspondence between common critical comments on Postmodernism and the synonyms for, and senses of, "Unreality."

UNREAL: non-existent; extinct, dead, lifeless, disassociated . . . from . . .reality, nihilistic; *illusory,* illusion, illusionistic, unreal, apparitions, silly, dreamlike, image, impression, holographic, "emperor's new clothes"; *ungenuine,* pretense, ungenuine, insincere, prententious, schizophrenic, "prose-puffed," "flying high on verbal vitamins," synthetic, reinvented, games, coded, joke, jokes, cruel joke, practical joke, stand-up joke, "ha, ha ha, hee hee hee, ho ho ho . . . oh no!", nostalgia, tongue in cheek, witty, plaything; *tenuous,* artificial, strained, vague, eccentric, ephemeral, throw-away, inaccessible, instant, evasion of substance, vacuous, airbrushed, askew, shallow, media-happening, high gloss, sensationalism, procrastinating; *idealization,* narcissistic, idealized visions, grandiose, intellectual, intellectual rationalization, intellectual exercise, esoteric, esoterica, academic, recondite, erudite, elite, elitist, cult.

ERRONEOUS: false, false, falsehood, unfair, plagiarize, preposterous, inappropriate, decadent, self-indulgent, crock, dishonest, "transient honesty," "design a lie," distorted, obscured (reality), teasing; *imperfect,* disorganized, contorted, crude, confused, overcomplex, biased, miscast, loony, naughty, undisciplined, chaotic, lack of discipline, warped, gimmick, blunder; *inaccurate,* unintended (meanings), ill-proportioned, scaleless, overscaled; *unorthodox,* awkward, deliberately awkward, violation, mannered, mannerism, odd, idiosyncratic, oddball, novel, novelty, exaggerated, hyperbole, bizarre, off-beat, campy, pop, misguided, perverted, inappropriate.

IMAGINARY: illusory, surrealistic, seductive pictorial, images, imagery, "architect as conjurer," "sleight-of-hand," drawings and models, "deliciously drawable," dreamland, "magic kingdom fantasias," and cf. *illusory* above; *tenuous,* abstract, high-minded, mysterious, sophistry, "clothes but no emperor," emptiness, and cf. *tenuous* above.

IMPOSSIBLE: fantastic, fantasy, shock, stunt, unbelievable, monstrosity, grotesque, convoluted, ludicrous, unnerving, absurd, outrageous, ridiculous, exaggeration, surreal, surrealism; *hopeless,* cowardly, resignation, disheartening, jettisoning ("social concern"), depersonalization, search (" . . . without knowing where to look"), depressing, loss (" . . . of faith," " . . . of professional ethic"), symbols of despair, escapism; *unacceptable,* inadequate, "what in the world is going on?," fascist, fascistic, futile, garbage, trash, visual pollution, ignoring ("environmental crisis"), ignores the realities, alienated, revolutionary, little concern for service, little understanding of nature/principles, failure to.

IMMATERIAL: non-material, ephemeral, intangible, transient, constant change, intentions (only), without substance; *irrelevant,* inconsequential, unrelated, meaningless, flashy, useless, product for consumption (?), flight from reality, frivolity/frivolous, "anachronistic foray," egocentric frivolity, exotic, private, "lifeless cliché," "jocular triteness," "devoid of real sense;" *unimportant,* picayune, one-dimensional, trivializing, facile, time-wasting, cheap thrills.

UNSUBSTANTIAL: frail, flimsy, cheap, "using history as a crutch," stageset, pasteboard, tinsel, shoddy, spindly transparency, shallow, cartoon-like, symbolic fragments, frosting, skin deep; *illogical,* ironic, unsettling, incongruous, gibberish, nonsense, "conglomerate of visual nonsense", senseless, petulant, disregard of (the) actual, irrational, irrational rituals, fissionistic, contraption, whimsy, arbitrarily elegant; *intangible,* abstraction, empty, vacuum, openendedness, effect, without substance, verbalization, paper structures; *unreliable,* silly, boondoggle, "short lived genre art," insane, interlude, temporary, fickle, "promises but fails to deliver . . . ," uncontrolled (mannerism); *weak,* "impoverished sense of time," unimaginative, poor, effete, impoverished symbols, banal, half-baked, glutinous [prose], small.

INAUTHENTIC: artificial, contrived, forced, placebo; *illogical* fancied exigencies, and cf. above; *unauthoritative,* trite, connotations, gestures, indiscriminate projection, preoccupation with visual, inauthentic, "too easy," glib, populist, cliché, digressive, latest trends, jargon of fashion, obscure academic gestures, obfuscating, "no program, no site, and no client projects," "writing history rather than making it," harmless fun, hype, camp, "interior decorators who work in the rain."

NON-IDENTITY: non-buildings, non-architecture, out of context, potpourri, montage, anachronism, "collectage", eclecticism, pastiche, ubiquitous, fragments, superimposition, divorced, hodge-podge, bewildering, pluralism, pluralistic, costuming; *ambiguous,* ambiguous, no relation, mutation, incongruity, confused.

IMITATION: borrowing, misappropriated shards; *copy,* copies, copying incessantly, simulated [ruins]; *duplication,* replica; *facsimile,* exessive imitation, translations; *fake,* tricky, fake; *impersonation,* costume ball, high drama, "elitism masquerading as populism", disguise; *repetition,* redundant extravagance, collections of . . . , obsessive; *reproduction,* (capricious) recreation, banal transposition of . . . signs; *ridicule,*mimic, buffoonery, caricature, "little Jack Horner syndrome"; *similarity,* metaphors, comparison, allude, allusions, references; *simulation,* movie set, calculated stageset, stageset design; *mock,* puns, funnies, farce, parodies, lampoon, spoof, mockery, amusing, "hysterical historicism," painted icons, side show, "gross debasement," disdain (-ful); *ungenuine,* "fear of the straight-forward," "semantic flapdoodle," "neofashion," affection, euphemisms, and cf. above.

APPEARANCE: apparition, "multiform apparition"; *exteriority,* masked, decorative, decoration, "Greek temples glued on . . . ," facade, packaging, props, stick-on flourishes, titillating packages, "gravely obfuscated embellishism," layering, flat, superficial, appliqués, fashionable, theatrical, set, "anything goes" look, slapped on, only trappings; *facade, fakery,* mock-ups, cut-outs, and cf. above; *form,* sculpture, superficial form, "monument over matter," form rather than substance, "visual nifties"; *illusoriness,* soundstage walls, photorealism; *specter,* unbearable, coarse image, hoax.

NOTES

1. Venturi, Rauch and Scott-Brown, "House in New Castle City, De.", *Progressive Architecture* (January 1980) 104.

2. Paul Horgan, *Whitewater* (New York: Farrar Straus Giroux, 1970) 163. Also cited in Yi-Fu Tuan, *Space and Place* (Minneapolis: Minnesota UP, 1977) 142.

3. Robert Hass, *Field Guide* (New Haven: Yale UP, 1973).

4. John Gardner, *On Moral Fiction* (New York: Basic, 1978).

5. There is also a literature that *aspires* to the condition of unmediated reality. "The reading of a fine poem or story or novel which holds us by its power is full of mysterious joys and frustrations. There is a sense of carnal delight, images of being . . . an 'illusion of reality' of scene or person so intense that we feel we are voyaging. . . . [This] delight is mingled with the awakening of spiritual expectation, the desire for 'meaning'—but as we read we do not question . . . the larger measure of the unmeaningful. We find ourselves in a landscape . . . [in] which all things vibrate with their own presence, and nothing—no matter how fantastic—is so unreal as to 'mean'." Millicent Bell, "Henry James, Meaning and Unmeaning," *Raritan* (Fall 1984) 30.

6. Susan Sontag, *Against Interpretation* (New York: Dell, 1966) p. 20.

7. . . . courtesy Heisenberg's "Uncertainty Principle," surely the most quoted, least understood, worst applied notion from physics to the human sciences since Einstein's Theory of General Relativity.

8. William James, *Principles of Psychology,* (New York: Dover, 1950).

9. Erving Goffman, *Frame Analysis,* (Cambridge, MA.: Harvard UP, 1974).

10. Arthur C. Danto, *The Transfiguration of the Commonplace,* (Cambridge, MA.: Harvard University Press, 1981.)

11. " . . . the question of 'deceit' is one rather of degree than principle, rather of experiment than law." Geoffrey Scott, *The Architecture of Humanism,* (New York: Norton, 1974) 122; also see 114-122.

12. Cf. Benedetto Gravagnuolo, *Adolf Loos: Theory and Works* (New York: Rizzoli International, 1982).

13. Buildings under construction form the inverse case to ruins: their constitutive materiality is as clearly evident. Furthermore, the ad hoc air of construction equipment—uncomposed yet practical—the often unusual yet explicable light conditions as sun streams through studs, steel, and half-made roofs, the rain that falls in unsuspected places, and the smells of sawn wood and welding and cement . . . these and the incomplete state of the building as such, all lend presence and both emptiness$_1$ and emptiness$_2$ to the structure. (For the architects, the clients, the builder, involved so deeply with the building, significance too, of course, is a major factor.) Liking a building more at various points

during the construction process than after its completion is a common experience (at least for architects) and not surprising: the realness seduces. The esthetic of "incomplete construction" fairly guides the work of Frank Gehry, while careful detailing and execution of inexpensive lumber-yard materials left natural—showing the same desire for materiality—has become a trademark of some of his younger Los Angeles contemporaries.

14. Popular Zen poem, unattributed; my own 17-syllable haiku version.

15. Gravagnuolo, 78-82.

16. John Dewey, *Art as Experience* (New York: Minton Balch, 1934).

17. Czeslaw Milosz, *Native Realm: A Search for Self Definition* (New York, Doubleday, 1981), cited in *Newsweek* (9 February 1981), 88.

18. "I have an idea . . . and I think it tells a lot about this country. . . . The greatest man-made beauties in America are industrial accidents! Most everything else they try to make beautiful is awful. But now and then something wonderful comes out of factories, or streetlamps, or railroads, or grain elevators, and that is some kind of art. I don't know what kind. But it does the same thing as art. And nobody means it to!" Philip Durham in Horgan, 165. This passage immediately follows the one cited at the beginning of this essay.

19. We should not groan at the proposal—if not yet arrival—of a new "-ism." It is in the nature of esthetic ideas and styles to succeed and replace each other. Like a shark that must move to keep from suffocating, or, to switch metaphors, like water cut by the prow of a ship to arc clear into the air, esthetic vision is released by the passing of the mind at new angles through the objects being contemplated. Born with no choice in the matter into a ready-made world, man never tires of confirmation that he is indeed alive and that he deserves to be here. All new styles—in clothes, furniture, graphics, architecture, literature, art, even the human sciences—all new styles and apologias and theories (like this one) are attempts to sharpen our perception, to awaken us to the world and to make our existence in it more vital. Excursions from reality are just that: excursions from which we might return refreshed, to "see again," and do not prove by their very existence that reality is intrinsically dull and meaningless. We could not bear to live long believing this except drugged. On the contrary, the reality we sense to be different from our dreams and imaginings is never exhausted. No genuine solace can be found in escape from a reality so rich in order and subtle in its ways; nor can any entertainment please that ignores its ancient color and meter.